At sea

Gannet
This beautiful bird is usually seen off shore rearing up into the sky and then diving headlong into a shoal of fish - hitting the water at as much as 30 m.p.h. Breeds on islands off the Welsh coast.

Puffin
This ... bird ... on ... the ... suc... Scilly Rock. Special boat trips are often arranged to watch these birds. Can be seen from Spring to the end of July.

Manx Shearwater
Superbly adapted for a life at sea skimming the tops of waves but completely unable to land gracefully on shore. Its landing technique simply seems to involve colliding with the ground. There are special boat trips to watch them as they come to land in the evening on Annet. There is a great cacophony as they establish the whereabouts of their mates and burrows.

European Storm Petrel
Breeds on Annet but are rarely seen during the day, except when it comes inshore to shelter from an oncoming storm - hence its name and reputation as a sign of bad weather to come.

Rocky habitats

Cormorant & Shag
Closely related species. The cormorant has a white face patch. The shag is one of the most commonly spotted birds - especially in the shallow water between the islands where it sits on the surface, periodically diving to chase fish underwater. Usually spotted standing on rocks and buoys in this characteristic pose - drying out its wings between fishing trips.

Kittiwake
Spends most of the year out at sea. Breeds on sheltered cliff faces on Tresco & some of the other smaller islands.

Razorbill
Breeds in crevices between rocks on the more inhospitable islands. A member of the auk family.

Guillemot
Increasingly rare auk. Breeds on exposed rocky ledges on Men-a-vaur.

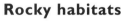

Great Black Backed Gull
Definitely a bird with 'attitude'. The charcoal back and wings give it a regal presence. It rarely seems to bother with human scraps instead preferring to feed on other birds and their chicks.

Herring Gull
The most common gull on our coasts and a prolific scavenger. It has adapted well to take advantage of the rubbish thrown away by man.

VISITOR INFORMATION

The Isles of Scilly lie about 30 miles southwest of Land's End in Cornwall. There are five inhabited islands all with accommodation. St Mary's is the main island. Although there are roads on the islands it is not possible to bring your own car to Scilly.

Isles of Scilly Tourist Information Centre

Hugh Town, St Mary's. T(01720) 422536 E tic@scilly.gov.uk **www.simplyscilly.co.uk**

HOW TO GET TO THE ISLANDS

Frequent daily trains run directly to Penzance from London Paddington, the north of England and Scotland . A sleeper service operates from London Paddington but as we go to print this service is under threat. **www.thetrainline.com**

Helicopter

Flights leave from the Heliport just outside Penzance. There is a connecting bus service from the train station to the heliport & secure parking is provided on site. Direct flights are available to St Mary's Airport and Tresco - the flight lasts about 20 mins. T(01736) 363871 **www.islesofscillyhelicopter.com**

Ship

The Scillonian III leaves from the Lighthouse Pier at Penzance Harbour. Long stay parking is available on the Harbour public car park opposite Penzance train station. Private secure parking is also available near the harbour. The trip takes about 2 hours 40 minutes. T 0845 710 5555 **www.ios-travel.co.uk**

Plane

The Isles of Scilly Skybus operate services from Newquay, St Just (9 miles from Penzance) & other UK airports to St Mary's Airport. A connecting bus service runs from Penzance train station. The flight lasts about 15 minutes. T 0845 710 5555 **www.ios-travel.co.uk**

ACTIVITIES

Sailing & Diving Tuition

Sailing tuition is available on most of the islands and there are diving centres on St Mary's & St Martin's. Contact the TIC for more information (see above).

Shipman Head

Bryher

Scilly Rock

Norrard

Norrard Rocks Gweal Hotel

Maiden Bower

Illiswilgig

Samson

Mincarlo

White Island

N O R T H C H A N N E L

Gt Mina

B R O A D S O U N D

Old Wreck Buoy

Gunners

Crim Rocks

Annet Lower Town

Hellweathers

Gt Crebawethan

St Agnes

Bishop Rock Lighthouse

Western Rocks

Melledgan

Rosevear

Rosevean Gorregan

Gilstone

GETTING AROUND THE ISLANDS

There is a frequent inter-island boat service between all the inhabited islands. The boats leave just after 10am in the morning and again at about 2pm in the afternoon. Return boats leave at lunchtime and late afternoon. Exact times and landing places are dependent on the tides (see individual island maps for details). On landing the boatman will let you know where he will pick you up. Other special excursions are common - to see the seals at the Western Rocks and Eastern Isles or to go puffin spotting at sea. There are also popular evening trips to the Turk's Head on St Agnes. Notice boards on each island display the departure times and destinations of that day's and the next day's sailings. You can also book special trips to uninhabited islands for the day. Annet and some other islands with large populations of birds are closed to visitors during the breeding season.

Pilot Gig Racing

Pilot gigs are six oared boats developed in the C19th to race competing pilots out to British bound sail ships. The first pilot to reach the ship would get the job to navigate it into port. This led to an intense rivalry between boats. The pilots are no longer required but the rivalry continues. Races happen every Wednesday and Friday evening in the Summer. Each island has its own boats & you can follow the race from a launch. The world championships are often held on Scilly, usually in May. The most common courses are from Nut Rock (Samson) to St Mary's and from Old Wreck Buoy (Annet) to St Mary's.

The Isles of Scilly

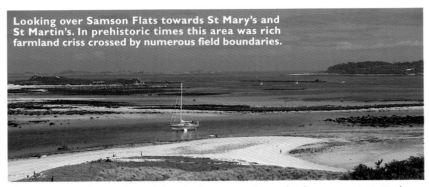

Looking over Samson Flats towards St Mary's and St Martin's. In prehistoric times this area was rich farmland criss crossed by numerous field boundaries.

There is something about islands that appeals to the human spirit. Perhaps it is the feeling of a world drawn at a smaller scale - everything on Scilly seems a step down in size from the mainland. Even the birds, so wary on the mainland, are tame enough to eat out of your hand here. This gives you a wonderfully refreshing feeling of walking in an enchanted landscape. Children instinctively respond to this and love the Isles of Scilly. If there is a currency in happy childhood memories then the islands are certainly rich.

Life on Scilly, as on all islands, is governed by the sea and the tides. It dictates the practicalities of both leisure and business. This is especially true of the smaller off-islands which are inaccessible by boat on a low Spring tide. Although surprisingly on this sort of tide you can actually walk between some of the islands across the exposed sand banks. As a result, life on the islands is as much centered on the lunar clock that controls the tides, as the 24 hour clock. The sea around the islands is in a constant state of change and motion. The tide can drop by as much as five metres in just six hours. That roughly equates to two billion tons of water on the move just in and around Scilly and accounts for the fierce currents that can race between the islands.

The heightened sense of the natural world is also evident in the way weather rolls in over the sea. Showers sweep across the sky and the horizon is always changing - sometimes sharply defined between sea and sky and sometimes melded into one. This awaking of the senses is nowhere more obvious than in the fabulous night skies on Scilly. There is hardly any pollution to reduce the clarity of the stars. The dusty band of the Milky Way is crystal clear and rolling home from the pub it sometimes feels as if you are being bombarded by shooting stars.

The five inhabited islands of Scilly all have their own character and you will soon find the island that suits you best. The three off-islands of St Agnes, Bryher and St Martin's are the most remote. Here the only traffic on the small concrete roads is the occasional tractor. Bryher feels the most rugged and will appeal to the romantic.

St Agnes is the most self contained and is said to appeal to the independent minded. St Martin's with its lush crescent bays and long beaches has a

serene feel to it. Tresco and St Mary's are more of a halfway house between the mainland and the off-islands with 'proper' traffic and more day trippers but to call them 'busy' or 'crowded' would be ridiculous. Tresco has the world famous Abbey Gardens. St Mary's is perfect for the first time visitor as all the other islands are within easy reach by inter-island launch.

Lyonnesse and the drowned landscape

The granite mass that forms the Isles of Scilly is part of a chain of dome like intrusions of granite that run from Dartmoor in the east, to the undersea outcrop of Haig Frais 40 miles northwest of the islands. These massive underground intrusions all occurred in response to a collision between continental plates in the earth's crust between 200 and 300 million years ago. The collision resulted in the formation of the Laurasian Mountains. The Scillonian granite was implanted and cooled many kilometres beneath these mountains and as the peaks were eroded away over the eons the granite has become exposed at the surface. Granite forms a distinctive landscape characterised by the towering carns that mark almost every headland. The granite here weathers into extraordinary shaped formations - most with their own names. Many formations such as the *Loaded Camel Rock* at Porth Hellick and the rocks of Peninnis Head on St Mary's mimic the shapes of animals or faces. Perhaps the most well known is the *Nag's Head* on St Agnes (see section on St Agnes). Inland, the granite soils are free draining but generally poor in nutrients and have to be 'sweetened' by shell sand and rotted seaweed to be productive.

Sea level has varied tremendously over geological time - falling levels being associated

5

The Loaded Camel Rock above Porth Hellick on St Mary's. Other strange shaped rocks on the islands include the Pulpit, Monk's Cowl and Tooth Rock at Peninnis Head on St Mary's. See also photo of the Nag's Head in the section on St Agnes.

with periods of glaciation where vast quantities of water become locked up in ice sheets. At the height of the most recent glaciation, 18,000 years ago sea level was as much as seventy five metres below the present day level and ice sheets extended from the north pole to cover half of Britain.

Generations of Scillonians have been told of a lost land that once lay between the Isles of Scilly and Land's End - the land of Lyonnesse. A land it is said, of handsome maids and strong men; of rich pastures and fertile meadows and the beautiful city of Lions. A turreted castle stood on what is now the Sevenstones reef (halfway between land's End and Scilly) and from the highest turret you could count the steeples of 140 graceful churches. All this was suddenly engulfed by the sea. Sometimes late at night in the corner of a West Cornwall pub you may even overhear an old fisherman recounting stories of how on a calm day, with a still sea, you can just hear a mournful toll as the sea currents gently move the bells in their steeples. Only one man and his horse survived the sudden inundation. He was out hunting in the hills near to the present day Land's End. Weary from his exertions he fell asleep under a May tree only to be woken by a deep rumble that quickly grew into a terrifying roar as a gigantic wave rolled across the land from the west. He mounted his horse and they galloped for their lives up the slope to high ground and safety but not before the horse lost a shoe in the scramble. There is a family in West Cornwall today whose coat of arms consists of three horseshoes and they claim to be directly descended from the single survivor of the flood that engulfed Lyonnesse.

The legend may have grown taller with every telling but there are indeed traces of a lost society, their homes and fields now under the sea. We now know these are the homes of Bronze Age Scillonians who colonised Scilly 4,000 years ago when the four largest present day islands were connected by a now submerged central plain. Even today it is possible to wade between Tresco and Samson on a low Spring tide in August (see previous page). The tales of the fishermen must have been fuelled by seeing these submerged round houses and field walls. They now lie, tumbled and seaweed covered underwater between the islands and can also be seen on the foreshore of Green Bay on Bryher and at Pentle Bay on Tresco.

Innisidgen Neolithic/Bronze Age Entrance Grave on the north of St Mary's. This type of tomb is only found in Scilly and West Cornwall.

The first Scillonians

We know from archaeological finds of flint arrow heads that the first humans to reach Scilly were the Mesolithic peoples (8000BC-4000BC). They moved north from the Mediterranean after the end of the last ice age 10,000 years ago probably following herds of migrating animals as the ice retreated. We have little evidence of how these people lived except that they may have lived a semi-transient life rather like native American Indians of the C19th. If they did roam here then most of their camps are now lost to the sea and there is little trace of them on the present islands. At the start of the Mesolithic Age there was probably still enough water held in the ice caps for Scilly to still be connected to the mainland but by 4000BC Scilly had become a single island, with a wooded interior populated with deer and wild boar.

The Neolithic peoples (4000BC-2500BC) are the first people to really leave a mark on the landscape. They lived a more settled life, cultivating cereals, domesticating animals as well as hunting and gathering. They shared a common culture with the other peoples of the Atlantic seaboard from Spain, Brittany through Cornwall to Wales and Ireland. It was these people that built the first tombs and monuments in the landscape. In West Cornwall they built the large 'table like' quoits such as Lanyon and Mulfra Quoit near Penzance. Some of the entrance graves so characteristic of Scilly probably have their origins in this period and there is some evidence to suggest that Scilly was cultivated in a very limited way at this time.

It's not until the Bronze Age (2,500BC-700BC) that the islands seem to

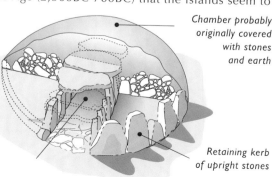

Chamber probably originally covered with stones and earth

Cremated remains placed in urns within passage. There is also some evidence of offerings of food and produce. Any precious grave goods have long been stolen.

Retaining kerb of upright stones

Bronze Age Entrance Grave

7

The Bronze Age entrance Grave on Buzza Hill looking over Porthcressa and Hugh Town towards the Garrison

come under sustained and widespread cultivation. The land was cleared of stones some piled in circular mounds or cairns as on Shipman Head Down on Bryher. They cut down the wild wood and settled in villages of small round houses or hut circles. The stone foundations of these houses are common throughout the islands (although often hidden by bracken) and also show up as seaweed covered circles in the sandy, shallow sea between the islands. They are particularly obvious when seen from the helicopter as it comes in to land at Tresco.

It was these people who built the entrance graves that sit on almost every hilltop on the islands Over seventy examples are documented on the islands. This is a type of tomb is only found in Scilly and West Cornwall and they echo the more elaborate passage graves of Ireland and Brittany. They are often aligned together in 'family' groups on the crests of prominent hills such as North & South Hill on Samson, Cruther's Hill on St Martin's, the north end of Gugh and on Porth Hellick Down on St Mary's. The best individual examples are at Innisidgen and Porth Hellick Down on St Mary's. There is evidence of both cremation, with the remains placed in pottery urns and simple internment with the bodies allowed to disintegrate naturally. This probably reflects that the entrance graves were in use over long periods. Entrance graves are often found linked by low field walls and it has been suggested that they may have had a function associated with fertility of the soil, perhaps in response to the exhaustion of the soil by poor farming practice. Towards the end of the Bronze Age cairns took over from entrance graves as the preferred funeral monuments. Cairns are essentially mounds of stones and they sometimes have a burial cist at their centre. Shipman Head Down on Bryher has an exceptionally large number of cairns. Other typical Bronze Age monuments are standing stones or menhirs. The best known on Scilly is the Old Man of Gugh, but there are several others including a statue menhir on Chapel Down, St Martin's.

During the Iron Age (700BC-400AD) there developed a sophisticated improvement on the common round house called the courtyard house. Once again, this type of building is unique to Scilly and West Cornwall. There is a good example at Halangy Ancient Village on St Mary's. Cliff castles also date from this period - there are no spectacular examples on the islands but there are visible remains at the Giant's Castle on St Mary's and at Shipman Head on Bryher. In the later period of the Iron Age Rome ruled Britain. This appears to have had a limited impact on the day to day lives of Celts in this remote part of Britain. The Romans seem to have upheld the Celtic status quo and Iron Age culture continued to develop unhindered. In Scilly there seems to have been frequent contact with Roman trading ships. A Roman altar can be seen in the Abbey Gardens on Tresco and a Romano-British shrine was discovered on Nornour after storms exposed the remains of round houses at the head of the beach. The shrine was probably dedicated to a maritime goddess. In 387AD two early Christian Bishops, Instantius and Tibericus were exiled here from Rome for the Prissillian heresy. They headed a cult of free love and of course being bishops, they insisted they got more free love, more often, than anyone else. When they arrived in Scilly they probably found that if Christianity had taken root here at all - it had already died out.

The departure of the Romans from Britain in C5th precipitated a slow decline in trade and commerce. The country split into a number of fractious small kingdoms. Christianity, which had spread from Rome had also declined but was reestablished by missionaries from Wales and Ireland in the C7th and C8th, where it had always remained strong. The Celtic Christian tradition is a very different tradition to the Church of Rome and is much more based around hermits and small monastic settlements more typical of the Eastern Church. These men and women later became the Celtic saints and founded a number of small chapels on the islands (see sections on St Helen's and Tean). The greatest threat to the way of life would have been the gradual rise in the sea level, with storms and storm surges inundating the low lying central plain of Ennor. At sometime around the year 1000 the existing islands began to emerge from the sinking Isle of Ennor. The population of the islands at this point had probably fallen to a few hundred - many of those living a hand to mouth existence.

In 1120 Henry I granted all the churches on the northern part of Ennor to the Benedictine monks of Tavistock Abbey. The southern half of St Mary's and Agnes were granted to the Norman knight Richard de Wika. At this time Vikings and raiders from Ireland were a constant menace and eventually prompted the abandonment of Tresco Priory. Edward III granted the islands to the Black

Longstone standing stone on St Mary's

9

Prince, the first Duke of Cornwall, but Scilly was plagued by the twin threats of insecurity and the loss of the best agricultural land to the sea. For the next 400 years the islands seem to have sunk into obscurity.

The growth of sea trade on the new Atlantic trade routes to America and Africa from the Tudor period onwards brought the islands to the attention of national government. In order to safeguard the strategic position of Scilly fortifications were started and in 1570 the islands were leased by the Duchy to the Godolphin family. At this time the islands were used as a base for privateers raiding the heavily laden ships heading home with valuable booty. In Elizabethan times this piracy was ignored as long as it was to the detriment of Holland and France. However the Spanish Armada had shown how vulnerable the islands were to attack and so in 1593 Elizabeth I started to build the Star Castle on the Garrison.

During the English Civil War the islands were staunchly Royalist and Prince Charles stayed in the Star Castle in his flight from the Parliamentary forces in 1646. After subjugation by Parliament the islands rebelled in 1648 and took up attacking passing merchantman once more. In 1651 the toll on Dutch shipping prompted their government declare war on the islands - an act that was only withdrawn 20 years ago when the Dutch ambassador visited the islands to formally declare peace. After the end of the Civil War Parliament encouraged a period of resettlement by families from the mainland.

By the end of the C18th and the beginning of the C19th life on Scilly was again at a low ebb. The Napoleonic Wars disrupted smuggling and fishing, both major sources of income for Scillonians. A series of poor harvests following the end of the Napoleonic wars brought a real prospect of famine. Pilotage fees for ships sailing to the major British ports gave some help but it was not enough to stop the islands falling into destitution. It fell to a visionary man called Augustus Smith to turn the situation around. He obtained the lease from the Duchy of Cornwall after the Godolphin family relinquished it in 1831 and set about reform. He insisted that the children should be well educated, a legacy continued to this day and he introduced new agricultural practices. The growth of the railways in the middle of the C19th brought the first tourists to the islands and also allowed the flower industry to flourish. For the first time cut flowers could now reach the London markets within a day and Scilly could exploit its early flowering season by supplying the London markets in the Winter.

Political instability in Europe at the beginning of the C20th caused the Government, ever mindful of the strategic position of the islands, to build new coastal batteries on the Garrison. During the First World War flying boats were stationed at Tresco and during the Second World War a squadron of Hurricanes were stationed on St Mary's to provide cover for convoys coming across the Atlantic.

Further reading: *The Archaeology of Scilly* Cornwall Archaeological Unit
Exploration of a Drowned Landscape by Charles Thomas

St Mary's

> **Ferry**
> Inter-island ferries leave from the Old Pier near the Scillonian III berth. Boats usually leave at about 10am and 2pm - depending on the tide. Information boards giving details and times of sailings can be found in Hugh Town and at the Old Pier.
>
> **Best things to do**
> **Halangy Iron Age Village** - Excavated prehistoric settlement with Bronze Age entrance grave and Iron Age houses. **Island Museum** - Artifacts collected from the prehistoric sites of Scilly and from the wrecks that have foundered here. **Longstone Heritage Centre** - Exhibits from the local and maritime history of the islands. **Best Beaches** - Pelistry and Porth Minick are popular.

St Mary's is the largest island in the Scillonian group. It's the ideal place to be based on your first trip to the islands as all the other smaller islands are easily accessible from here by inter-island boat service from the quay in Hugh Town - the main settlement with the majority of the shops, pubs and restaurants on the island. St Mary's is a halfway house between the mainland and the more remote off-islands such as Bryher and St Agnes. There are even places on St Mary's where you can't see the sea, which is most unusual on Scilly and probably explains why some off islanders regard St Mary's with the same sort of disdain they reserve for the mainland. Cars and buses are common on St Mary's whereas on the off-islands tractors are the preferred form of transport. The sheltered centre of the island is mainly cultivated for flowers, particularly daffodils and narcissi which are sent to London in the Winter and early Spring. Vegetables and especially early potatoes are also widely cultivated.

It's possible to walk the coast of St Mary's in a single day but unless you are a seasoned walker it's probably better to split the island up into smaller more manageable parts that can be covered in a single afternoon. The island bus service can drop you at the north end of the island so that you can then walk half the coast in either direction back to Hugh Town. In addition to the coast there are nature trails at Lower and Higher Moors. The Isles of Scilly Environmental Trust produce leaflets on the plant and birdlife on the trails. There are also popular evening strolls from Hugh Town to both Peninnis Head and the Garrison.

St Mary's has many impressive prehistoric monuments. Scilly was on the main sea routes between the Bronze Age cultures of the Atlantic seaboard stretching from Portugal and Spain in the south to Ireland and Scotland in the north. Some of the most notable monuments are the exceptional Giant's Tomb on Porth Hellick Down, Innisidgen entrance grave on Helvear Down and Bant's Carn entrance grave on Halangy Down. Below Bant's Carn lies the later, more domestic scene of Halangy Down Iron Age village where you can wander around the 3,000 year old round houses.

When the low lying plain of the single prehistoric Isle of Ennor became submerged at about 1000AD St Mary's started to emerge as a separate island.

The now demolished Ennor Castle at Old Town became the principal seat of Norman civil administration and Old Town itself became the major port on the islands.

The growth of sea trade from the Tudor period and the strategic position of Scilly on the new Atlantic trade routes to America and Africa brought the islands to the attention of national government. In order to safeguard its position fortifications were started. The first was Harry's Walls above Porth Mellon where the new theories of gunnery angles and arcs of fire were implemented in the design of the bastion wall. However the site was poorly chosen and it gave only limited protection to shipping at anchor in St Mary's Road. It was abandoned before it was completed in favour of batteries on

Round island footpath   Porthloo   Telegraph

t Mary's
Pool

Mount Flagon/Harry's Wall's
Unfinished C16th Fortification

Porth
Mellon

Rose
Hill

A3111

ifeboat
;tation

Carn
Thomas

Normandy

Sandy Bank

Isles of Scilly
Secondary School

Lower Moors

Normandy

Moor Well

A3112

urch Street

Rams Valley

Church Road

Buzza Hill Entrance Grave
Bronze Age C25th BC-C7th BC

Carn Gwarvel
Primary School

Nature
Trail

Old Town

Castle Farm

Hospital
& Health
Centre

A3112

Nowhere

King Edward's Road

essa

rthcressa
Brow

Old Town
Church

Slip

Old Quay

Round island footpath

aven

icholl's
Rock

Carn Leh

Stony
Porth

Joe's
Rock

Carn
Mahael

Peninnis Mill
(ruin)

Carn Leh
Cove

Pulpit
Rock

Dutchman's
Carn

Peninnis
Head

The Chair
The Murrs

Tooth
Rock

Piper's
Hole

Inner Head

Monk's
Cowl

Little Jolly Rock

Pollard

Big Jolly Rock

Outer Head

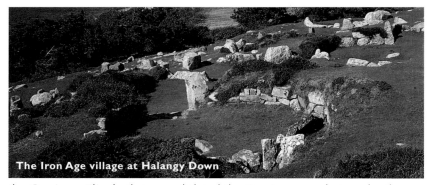

The Iron Age village at Halangy Down

the Garrison. Elizabeth I consolidated the Garrison as a fortress by the building of the Star Castle. The Star Castle was started in 1593 in response to the failed Spanish Armada of 1588. It's part of a chain of similar castles that stretch along the English south coast from Deal in Kent to Pendennis Castle at Falmouth. The Garrison walls were progressively added in Elizabethan times until the whole headland was effectively fortified. Hugh Town developed in the protective shadow of the castle during the C18th and C19th.

The main coastal footpath follows the later C17th & C18th walls that further fortified the Garrison against attack. The walls are punctuated at intervals by bastions designed to house batteries of cannon to prevent entry to the sheltered anchorage of St Mary's Road. Canons have been reinstated at King Charles Battery. At Woolpack Point you can take a short cut back to Hugh Town by climbing up the hill to Woolpack C19th Coastal Defence Battery. This was one of a series of batteries around the British coast that were built in 1900 in response to political instability and revolution in Europe. The battery became redundant along with all coastal batteries with the invention of the atomic bomb in the 1950's. The TIC have a leaflet that covers the archaeology and history of this walk in greater detail.

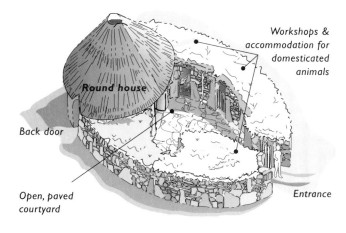

Workshops & accommodation for domesticated animals

Round house

Back door

Open, paved courtyard

Entrance

Reconstruction of an Iron Age Courtyard House.
Best examples - Nornour & Halangy Down Ancient Village.

St Mary's Island Walk

If you do not wish to walk the whole coast path you might decide to take the bus to the north end of the island and walk back to Hugh Town via Porth Hellick and Old Town. It would be worth taking a pasty or lunch with you to eat at Innisidgen or Watermill Cove. Best place to stop for a swim is Pelistry Bay.

Distance: *5 miles round trip (3-4 hours).* **Bus:** *Island bus service leaves from The Parade in Hugh Town.*
Pub/Refreshments: *Cafes at Porthloo, Old Town, Carn Vean & Hugh Town. Pubs in Hugh Town.*
Walk along the Strand following the road past the school & lifeboat house to Porth Mellon. Take the coast path above the beach to Harry's Walls.

Mount Flagon & Harry's Walls
Abandoned soon after it was started in 1551 because it was poorly sited for the use of cannons. The builder had obviously not quite understood the principles behind the new weapon technology of the C16th. A Bronze Age menhir stands below the shipping daymark.

Halangy Down Ancient Settlement & Bant's Carn Entrance Grave
The very fine entrance grave is one of the best examples on the islands and dates from the late Stone Age/early Bronze Age. The settlement of round houses and a single courtyard house are later, dating from the Iron Age. A booklet is available from the Custodian giving a detailed history and explanation of the site.

Innisidgen Entrance Graves
Another good Bronze Age entrance grave, perhaps as much as 4,500 years old.

Pelistry Bay & Toll's Island
Favourite beach for many on St Mary's and good place for a family day out. Beware of the tidal currents when the bar is covered. Toll's Island has the remains of Civil War gun platforms and on the south of the island a string of kelp pits used to burn seaweed to make soda and potash for the glass industry.

Porth Hellick Down
A concentration of entrance graves including the very large and fine example of the Giant's Tomb - the largest entrance grave on Scilly.

Old Town
Formerly *Porthennor* - the original Early Medieval settlement at a time when the present day islands were just starting to emerge from the single isle of Ennor. Barely anything survives of the C13th Ennor Castle, the early Medieval administrative centre of the islands. It was demolished and robbed of stone when the Star Castle was constructed in the C16th. A Medieval pier is visible at low water as a curve of jumbled rocks and a Medieval granite trough sits nearby for salting and preserving fish.
Cafe at Old Town. If you would like to return to Hugh Town follow the road at the head of the beach.

Peninnis Head
Popular place for an evening stroll. The granite has weathered into weird shapes. Look for the Pulpit Rock, The Monk's Cowl, Tooth Rock or make up your own names.

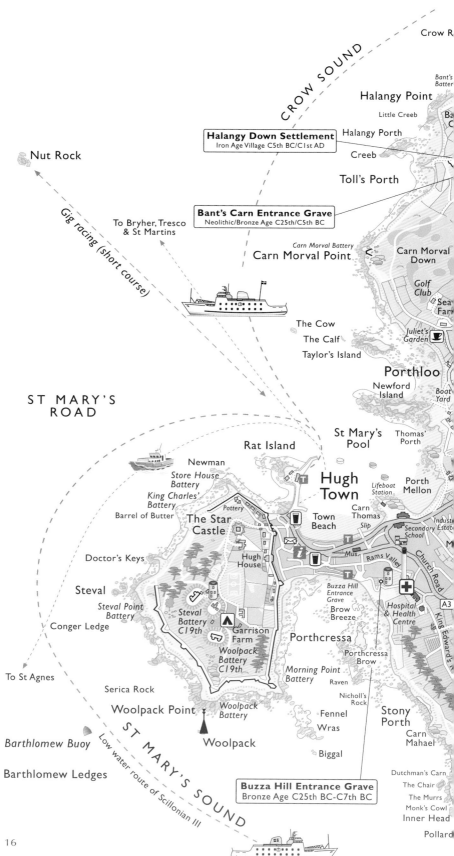

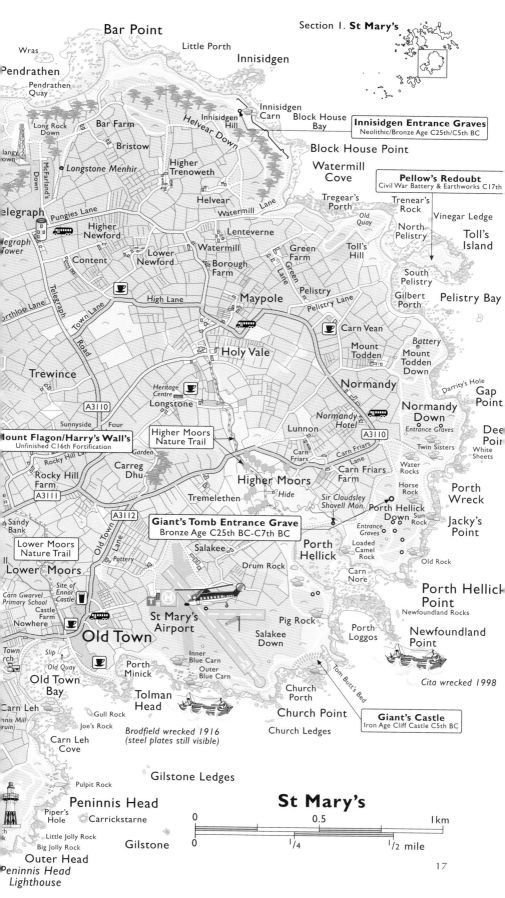

Bar Point

Wras

Little Porth

Innisidgen

Pendrathen

Pendrathen Quay

Long Rock Down

McFarland's

Bar Farm

Bristow

Longstone Menhir

Innisidgen Hill

Helyear Down

Innisidgen Carn

Block House Bay

Innisidgen Entrance Graves
Neolithic/Bronze Age C25th/C5th BC

Block House Point

Watermill Cove

Higher Trenoweth

Helvear

Helvear Lane

Watermill Lane

Lenteverne

Tregear's Porth

Old Quay

Trenear's Rock

Vinegar Ledge

North Pelistry

Toll's Island

elegraph

Telegraph Tower

Pungies Lane

Higher Newford

Content

Lower Newford

Watermill

Borough Farm

Green Farm

Green Lane

Toll's Hill

South Pelistry

legraph Tower

Down

Telegraph Road

Town Lane

High Lane

Maypole

Pelistry

Pelistry Lane

Gilbert Porth

Pelistry Bay

orthloo Lane

Holy Vale

Carn Vean

Mount Todden

Battery

Mount Todden Down

Trewince

Heritage Centre

Longstone

A3110

Normandy

Darrity's Hole

Gap Point

Sunnyside

Four

ount Flagon/Harry's Wall's
Unfinished C16th Fortification

Rocky Hill La

Higher Moors Nature Trail

Garden

Lunnon

Normandy Hotel

A3110

Normandy Down

Entrance Graves

Twin Sisters

White Sheets

Dee Poir

Rocky Hill Farm

A3111

Carreg Dhu

Tremelethen

Higher Moors

Hide

Carn Friars

Carn Friars Lane

Carn Friars Farm

Water Rocks

Horse Rock

Porth Wreck

Sandy Bank

A3112

Giant's Tomb Entrance Grave
Bronze Age C25th BC-C7th BC

Old Town Lane

Salakee

Pottery

Sir Cloudsley Shovell Mon.

Porth Hellick Down

Sun Rock

Jacky's Point

Lower Moors Nature Trail

Drum Rock

Porth Hellick

Entrance Graves

Loaded Camel Rock

Old Rock

Lower Moors

Carn Gwarvel Primary School

Site of Ennor Castle

Castle Farm

Nowhere

Old Town

St Mary's Airport

Pig Rock

Salakee Down

Carn Nore

Porth Loggos

Porth Hellick Point
Newfoundland Rocks

Newfoundland Point

Town rch

Slip

Old Quay

Porth Minick

Inner Blue Carn

Outer Blue Carn

Old Town Bay

Tolman Head

Church Porth

Tom Butt's Bed

Cita wrecked 1998

Carn Leh

arn Mill ruin

Gull Rock

Joe's Rock

*Brodfield wrecked 1916
(steel plates still visible)*

Church Point

Church Ledges

Giant's Castle
Iron Age Cliff Castle C5th BC

Carn Leh Cove

Gilstone Ledges

Pulpit Rock

Peninnis Head

St Mary's

Piper's Hole

Carrickstarne

Little Jolly Rock

Big Jolly Rock

Gilstone

Outer Head

eninnis Head Lighthouse

0   0.5   1km

0   1/4   1/2 mile

Higher Moors

Tremelethen

Maypole

Holy Vale

Normandy

Lunnon

Trewince

Watermill

Green Farm

Toll's Hill

Mount Todden

Pellow's Redoubt
Civil War Battery & Earthworks C17th

Section 2.
St Agnes & Gugh

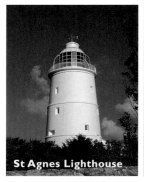

St Agnes Lighthouse

Food & Drink
St Agnes PO & Stores sells pasties and other provisions. The Turk's Head pub at Porth Conger is a popular eating place. Covean & Rose Cafes for tea and cakes.
Best things to do
Picnic on Periglis and look over to the Western Rocks & the Bishop Rock Lighthouse. Cove Vean about as perfect a beach as you will find - especially good for swimming.
Ferry
The ferry leaves from the quay at Porth Conger.

St Agnes and Gugh are the smallest and most self contained of the inhabited islands. They are separated from the rest of the group by the deep channel of St Mary's Sound. St Mary's and the other inhabited islands share the sheltered waters of The Road and Crow Sound and were still joined together as recently as 600 years ago. St Agnes has probably been a separate island for 1,000 years. The early separation from the other islands has allowed St Agnes to retain a strong Celtic flavour. It shares this with Samson and some of the more remote corners of West Cornwall with their Celtic holy wells and ancient superstitions and stories. In Celtic religion, wells and springs where thought to be a special conduit to the underworld - a sort of prehistoric cosmic wormhole. When Christianity became the dominant religion in the last centuries of the first millennium, the early Christians absorbed and recycled elements of the old religion. So the wells that once served for pagan religion became 'holy' wells renamed after Christian saints.

St Agnes has a fascinating example of this phenomenon in St Warna's Well, on the west side of Wingletang Down. The name Warna is unknown anywhere else as a Celtic saint and the origin may belong to one of the many savage Celtic water goddesses. Local tradition, dismissed for many years, said that offerings thrown into the well would 'ease' the passage of a ship onto the rocks. At one time shipwrecks were a vital additional income and resource for coastal communities. When the site was excavated this century a number of ancient gold pins were found at the bottom of the well. In fact St Agnes' position as the first landfall on the prevailing westerly winds has probably always given it a larger proportion of shipwrecks than the other islands. Such was the carnage in the C19th that the island had its own lifeboat stationed at Periglis from 1890 to 1920. The crew constituted 10% of population of the whole island. The grand lighthouse in the centre of the island no longer shows a light but it still serves as a daymark for shipping and because it's visible from all parts of St Agnes acts as a reference point for visitors. It was superseded by Peninnis Head Lighthouse on St Mary's.

Everyone has their favourite beaches on Scilly, but in Periglis, Cove Vean and The Bar, St Agnes has some of the loveliest. Periglis stretches out into the Atlantic and one can sit here and watch the Western Rocks submerge and resurface with the tide. Sometimes it really does feel like the last beach in the world. The white flakes of mica in the sand stick to the skin like fish scales and young children playing in the sand take on the appearance of mermaids. An appropriately Celtic transformation in a tradition where many of the wind sculpted rocks are named after animals and appear to come alive in the swirling sea mists that drift in from the Atlantic.

Cove Vean is more sheltered and perfect for exploring the foreshore at low water. The best walk on St Agnes is down Barnaby's Lane. In the Spring it is an oasis of lush vegetation and flowers on this otherwise exposed island. The Turk's Head pub at Porth Conger is one of the islands greatest assets. Residents from St Mary's often make the trip in the Summer for a drink which can be considered something of a miracle, as they rarely visit the off-islands.

The Gugh

Gugh like Samson, its physical twin, is rich in archaeological remains. It forms the end of a chain of hills starting from Samson Hill on Bryher, and passing through Samson itself, which seem to have had a special importance for the prehistoric inhabitants of Scilly. All these hills have alignments of large and impressive entrance graves on their summits - a sort of Beverly Hills of the prehistoric dead. They may have had added significance as prehistoric burial places because of the views over the sea to the setting sun - views which still make them popular places today. Many of the entrance graves on the islands - not just the hilltop ones, are set in places with impressive views. It seems reasonable to speculate that this was one of the most important characteristics of a site to ancient people - after all it is still important to us 3,000 years later.

Gugh is linked to St Agnes at low water by a sand and shingle bar - be sure to know the tide times when you set off, because apart from being marooned on the island, there are strong currents over the bar at high water which would make it unsafe to swim back. In the Summer the neck of Gugh is covered in a thick blanket of impenetrable bracken but there is always a good path to Dropnose Porth, a popular sheltered place to swim, and up to the Old Man of Gugh an ancient standing stone. The southern end of Gugh is inhabited by breeding gulls in the Summer and is best avoided - apart from the disturbance to the birds you are likely to find yourself being dive bombed by irate parents as you approach the nest sites. The gulls have an uncanny accuracy with their fishy faeces that discourages most intruders.

The present human inhabitants have been on the island since the 1940's, when they constructed the barns that overlook The Cove. Before that, Gugh had probably been uninhabited since the Iron Age, 1,500 years ago. In Spring Iron Age hut circles are visible at Tol Tuppens and on the north east side of Kittern Hill. An alignment of late Bronze Age entrance graves and cairns crown Kittern Hill - they are joined by a contemporary stone field

Half Tide Ledges

Little Smith

Round Rock of Porth Coose

Milk Ledges

Little Perconger Ledges

Little Smith Brow

Browarth

Round Rock of Porth Killier

Cow & Calf

Tins Walbert

Porth Coose Carn

Kallimay Point

Tol Tupp

Porth Coose

Carn of Porth Killier

Porth Killier

Quay

Porth Conger

Ginamoney Carn

Burnt Island

Big Carn

Big Pool

Slip

Periglis

Lower Town Farm

Higher Town

The Ba

Little Carn

Blanket Bay

Old lifeboat slip

Lower Town

Middle Town

The Co

Gunner

Bergecooth

Tamerisk

Grinlinton Farm

Bergecooth Carns

Downs Farm

Cove Vean

Carns of Castella

Troy Town Farm

Nag's Head

Garabeara

Sacke Ro

Carnew Point

Castella Down

St Warna's Well

Carn of Cove Ve

Menglow

Maze

Beat Carn

Pink Carn

St Warna's Wel
Celtic Holy Well

Long Point

St Warna's Cove

St Warna's Carn

Carn Adnis

Boy's Rock

Rock

Cairns

Wingletang

Castle Vean

Saddle Ricky

Great Porth Warna

Punch Bowl

Wingletang Carn

Joggli Rock

Troy Town Maze
Celtic/Viking/C17th?

Little Porth Warna

Down

HMS Firebrand wrecked 1707

Little Porth Askin

Porth Askin

Beady Pool

Boy's Ro

Ragged Rock

Cairns

Pedn Brow

Lethegus Rocks

Gull Rocks

Grandfathe Hugh's Poin

Shooting Rock

Eastern Rock

The Beast

The Mare

St Agnes & Gugh

Horse Point

The Colt

Great Wingletang

0   0.5   1km

0   1/4   1/2 mile

The Nag's Head

Obadiah's Barrow Entrance Grave
Neolithic/Bronze Age C25th/C5th BC

The Old Man of Gugh
Bronze Age Menhir C15th/C5th BC

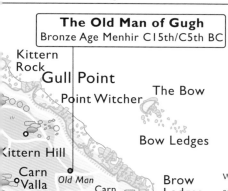

Kittern Rock

Gull Point

Point Witcher

The Bow

Bow Ledges

Kittern Hill

Carn Valla

Old Man

Carn Kimbra

Brow Ledges

The Barn

Dropnose Porth

The Gugh

Carn Bite

Carn Wrean

Dropnose Point

Carn of Works

Target Rock

Battery & Entrance Grave

Clapper of Works

The Flats

Hoe Point

The Hakestone

The Hoe

Little Hakestone

ean Plat Point

The Yellow Horned Poppy grows above Beady Pool

wall. This association has led to speculation about a possible link between the monuments and fertility. One theory suggests that the entrance graves were built because of a crisis in food production caused by poor cultivation methods. This would certainly go some way to explaining the extraordinarily large number of ancient monuments on Scilly. South east of Kittern Hill is the Old Man of Gugh, a Bronze Age menhir or standing stone. It has been standing here looking over what is now St Mary's Sound for the last 3,500 years. It is interesting to stand here and take a minute to think about how the landscape has changed since the stone was erected. When it was first put up, St Mary's Sound was probably a shallow cove sandwiched between the high land of the Garrison and Gugh. To the north lay a cultivated lowland plain with field walls and tree cover that stretched between all the existing islands. In 3,500 years time in AD5500, with the present rate of sea rise of about 3mm a year, the sea level will be about 10.5 metres higher than today. The waves will then be lapping at the base of the old man himself; the Garrison will be an island as will Peninnis Head and St Agnes will be a tiny island about 1/10 of the present size.

St Agnes Island Walk

St Agnes is easily walked in a morning and has more packed into its small size than any other island. If you want to simply sit and enjoy the view then Periglis is the best beach - if it's too windy try Cove Vean.

Distance: 3 miles round trip (2 hours). **Going:** Generally easy. **Refreshments:** Turks Head, Covean & Rose cafes.

From the quay walk towards the popular bird watching site of Big Pool.

Periglis & the old lifeboat station

From *Per*-cove and *eglos*-church. This was probably the site of an early Christian chapel. A lifeboat was first stationed here in 1890. The present lifeboat station· was built in 1903 and faces the Western Rocks - the site of a large number of wrecks. Many bodies from the loss of the Association, Eagle, Firebrand and Romney were buried here in 1707 (see Section 3 about the Western Rocks).

Bergecooth

Note the unusually vivid brick red granite on the foreshore.

Castella Down

In 1707 HMS Firebrand finally floundered on Menglow Rock just offshore after first hitting the Gilstone reef.

Troy Town Maze

There is some doubt as to age of this small maze - it was reinstated by a lighthouse keeper in the C19th, but may be much older. Similar mazes are found in Scandinavia and the Vikings certainly landed on Scilly to rape and pillage. In the C12th Orkneyingar Saga the Vikings mention the easy pickings that were to be had on Scilly.

The Nag's Head

This area forms part of the same band of granite that makes up Peninnis Head on St Mary's and in both places the granite forms strange animalistic shapes.

For a quick return to the post office and shop or if you need a cup of tea in a hurry, return to Downs & Middle Town by the track at the head of St Warna's Cove.

St Warna's Well

Tiny stone lined well dedicated to a pre Christian, presumably Celtic deity. It is said that in the past, islanders would drop offerings into the well to summon wrecks onto the shore when times were hard. When the site was excavated a number of gold pins and other votive offerings were found at the bottom of the well.

Wingletang Down

Most of the paths on the north of Wingletang Down lead to the huge loaf shaped rock called the Punchbowl. These large odd shaped rocks have a certain strange magnetism. There is almost always someone standing here just staring at the rock and you will probably find yourself doing exactly the same thing to no apparent end. In Cornwall in the C19th there were many such celebrity rocks, often popular sites for Sunday picnics. Unfortunately most have been quarried away.

Beady Pool

Ceramic beads from the wreck of a Venetian ship are sometimes washed onto the beach. Examples are on show at the Island Museum on St Mary's. Look out for the Yellow Horned Poppy at the head of the beach. Boy's rock was where the body of young lad was found.

Section 3.
The Western Rocks & The Bishop

Food & Drink
Remember to bring a picnic. There are no shops on the Western Rocks.
How to get there
Regular boat trips visit the Western Rocks and Bishop Lighthouse when the sea is not too rough. Occasionally a landing is possible on Rosevear to visit the old blacksmith workshop used during the construction of the Bishop Rock Lighthouse.
Wildlife
A boat trip to the Western Isles is often a good opportunity to watch the rarer seabirds that do not tend to come inshore. Seals also breed on the rocks.

The Western Rocks were known to seafarers over the centuries as the *Dogs of Scilly* and are one of the most notorious reefs on the Western Approaches. They have witnessed hundreds of wrecks and claimed thousands of lives - reportedly over 2,000 in one night alone when part of the British fleet foundered here in 1707. The prevention of disastrous wrecks was not helped by a long standing error in nautical charts that showed the rocks 10 miles further north before 1750. Added to that was a poorly understood sea current that tended to push shipping further north than expected. Navigation in the days of sail was an imprecise science. A captain could easily establish his position along a north/south line - his latitude by reference to the pole star in its constant position overhead. What he could not do with any accuracy was establish his position on an east/west line - his longitude. If it was cloudy all he could do was dead reckon - make an informed guess of his position based in the assumed speed and direction of the vessel.

The shock of the loss of the British Fleet on the Western Rocks in 1707 spurred the Admiralty to set a prize for the first person to find a reliable method of establishing longitude. This was theoretically straightforward. If you knew the time of midday at your departure point, you could measure the disparity between that, and the time of midday at your present position. In this way, the number of hours, minutes

The first Bishop Rock Lighthouse. Started in 1847 but washed away in 1850, before it could be commissioned.

Round Rock Buoy

Round Rock of Crebawethan

Condors Rocks

Great
Crebawethan

Little Crebawethan

Sprowse's
Brow

Wee

Crebawethan Neck
Round
Rock

Flat Ledge

The Bishop
Bishop Rock Lighthouse
The Clerk

Tearing Ledge

Cornish Ledge

Jacky's Rock

Tearing Ledge

Retarrier Ledges
Flat Ledge

Jolly Rock

The Ponds

Silver Carn

Santasperry Neck

Schiller wrecked 1875

Alastair's Rock

Crebinicks

Ruined Blacksmith's Workshop

Rosevear

Rosevear Neck

Rosevear Ledges

HMS Romney
wrecked 1707

Rosevean

Rosevean N

Isaac's Ledge

Daisy

Vin

The Gilstone
Gilstone Ledges

Black
Rock

HMS Association &
HMS Firebrand wrecked 1707

Old Bess

Pednathise
Head

and seconds could be translated into miles east/west of your starting point.
In combination with your latitude this gave you an exact position. The theory
was fine but the practice was very different. Clocks at this time were accurate
on land but because they were pendulum clocks, they could not keep time
on a ship that was pitching and rolling in the ocean. One man started to
work towards a solution. He was John Harrison, the son of a Yorkshire
carpenter and a master clockmaker. The rest of his life was spent working
on a spring based mechanism that would be unaffected by the motion of
a ship. This became known as Harrison's Chronometer and was the forerunner
of the pocket watch. Harrison eventually won the prize after a number of
sea trials proved the accuracy of his chronometer.

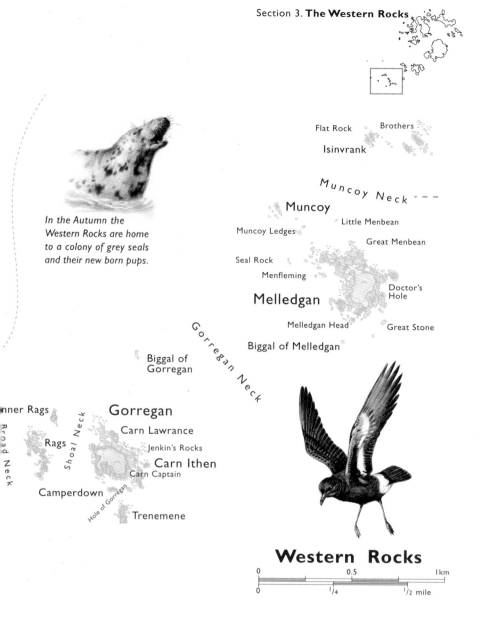

In the Autumn the Western Rocks are home to a colony of grey seals and their new born pups.

Flat Rock
Brothers
Isinvrank

Muncoy Neck

Muncoy
Little Menbean
Muncoy Ledges
Great Menbean

Seal Rock
Menfleming

Melledgan
Doctor's Hole

Melledgan Head
Great Stone

Biggal of Melledgan

Gorregan Neck

Biggal of Gorregan

Inner Rags

Broad Neck

Shoal Neck

Gorregan
Carn Lawrance
Rags
Jenkin's Rocks
Carn Ithen
Carn Captain

Camperdown

Hole of Gorregan

Trenemene

Western Rocks

| 0 | | 0.5 | | 1km |
| 0 | | 1/4 | | 1/2 mile |

The Bishop

The Bishop Rock has been performing the last rites on ships and crews ever since man first set sail in this part of the world. It is probably the most exposed of all the lighthouses around our coast. The rock itself is about 30 by 15 metres wide and is almost completely covered by a high Spring tide. It rises almost vertically from about 50 metres below sea level and so does not show the usual tell tale signs of breaking water that warn of a reef.

There are all number of explanations as to why the rock is called The Bishop. The most common is because of its similarity to the shape of a bishop's mitre. A more interesting one is that The Bishop and its near neighbour The Clerk, are named after two men found clinging to the rocks after a merchantman was wrecked here in C17th. The rocks were so isolated and little visited, that in those days the first indication of a wreck was often when bleached and bloated bodies started to wash ashore on St Agnes or at Porth Hellick on St Mary's. The threat to ships was so great that in 1680 one of the first lighthouses in Britain was constructed on St Agnes, but as it is 5 miles distant from the Bishop, and only had a weak light from a coal burning cresset, it was all but useless in fog and bad weather when it was most needed. For many years the difficult engineering task of putting a lighthouse on the Bishop, in such an exposed position was insurmountable. A design was finally agreed in 1847 and a blacksmith shop was set up on Rosevear. It took three years to construct and work was abandoned each Winter and resumed in the following Spring.

Cast iron columns were used in the hope that waves would simply pass through the structure. Keepers gained access to the accommodation via a central column. The whole structure was tied to the rock with huge cast iron bolts. On February 5th 1850, a storm simply washed the lighthouse from its base before it had even been commissioned. Prospective lighthouse keepers could have been forgiven for becoming rather apprehensive at the thought of serving on the Bishop.

Work restarted in 1858, this time on a design using a solid tower structure constructed from carefully dovetailed blocks of Cornish granite. This lighthouse saved lives even before it was completed. Survivors of a wreck were found one morning sheltering in the partially completed structure by a group of surprised masons. After completion it became almost immediately apparent that this structure was not strong enough to resist the very large waves to which The Bishop is subjected. Cracks were soon snaking up the sides of the tower and vibrations caused by the waves passing over the lighthouse made it shake violently, knocking plates and pots off the shelves. Apparently the

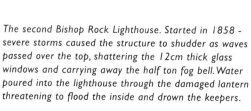

Fog Bell

The second Bishop Rock Lighthouse. Started in 1858 - severe storms caused the structure to shudder as waves passed over the top, shattering the 12cm thick glass windows and carrying away the half ton fog bell. Water poured into the lighthouse through the damaged lantern threatening to flood the inside and drown the keepers.

keepers were able to watch fish swim past the kitchen window 25 metres up. In April 1874 waves in excess of 40 metres high broke clear over the tower, washing away the lantern and bringing tons of water into the lighthouse, threatening to drown the keepers.

In 1881 an outer stone skin was built around the existing tower increasing its height and strength. Since then the structure has been without problems. The last keeper left in 1992 when the lighthouse became fully automated.

The wreck of the Association

Admiral Sir Cloudsley Shovell was one of the most celebrated sailors of his time. At the age of 15, during the Dutch War of 1665-7 he showed bravery that was later to become legendary by swimming between ships during a sea battle with battle orders in his mouth.

In 1707 the British fleet under Sir Cloudsley's command was returning from the Mediterranean where they had been fighting Barbary pirates. The fleet of 21 ships was hit by bad weather in the Bay of Biscay and become disorientated. Shovell called a meeting on his flagship HMS Association to try to reach agreement on their position. After much discussion they eventually agreed that they were well south of Scilly. Only one man dissented. He was a Scillonian by birth and said that he thought them to be only a few miles west of the islands. Later that night the fleet struck the Western Rocks. Four ships went down in quick succession. The next day, Sir Cloudsley's body was washed ashore at Porth Hellick - still alive. He was said to have been murdered where he lay by a local woman who wanted to steal his ring. His body was buried at the head of the beach. It was later exhumed, pickled in brandy and laid to rest in Westminster Abbey.

Lantern

Service Room

Engine Room

Bedroom

Living Room

Oil Room

Store Room

Entrance

Water Tank

Original wall of 2nd lighthouse

The third Bishop Rock Lighthouse. An outer casing sheathed the second weakened lighthouse.

Section 4.
Samson

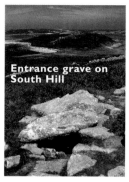

Entrance grave on
South Hill

Food & Drink
Remember to bring a picnic. There are no shops on Samson.
Best things to do
As well as the monuments on the island itself Samson is a great place from which to explore the life of the shallows and sandbanks. There are lots of small pools that trap fish and crabs on a outgoing tide. Look out for beautiful coloured cuttlefish and pipe fish.
Nesting birds
Some parts of the island are closed off in the Spring to protect nesting birds.

This small, now deserted island has an almost magical pull on many visitors and is often spoken of as the most vividly remembered part of any visit to the islands. It is a small but perfectly formed sensory masterpiece. Its twin hills and low lying neck form a neat figure of eight shape and give Samson a pleasing sense of serenity.

The concentration of prehistoric monuments on the twin hills suggest that it has been an important place since the islands were first settled in the Bronze Age and some archaeologists feel the settlement hidden beneath the sands of East Porth may have been one of the half dozen pioneer settlements in prehistoric times. At that time of course Samson was not an island, it was part of the much bigger single Isle of Ennor that took in almost all the present day islands. As the sea has submerged the land, the field walls that once penned in cattle in the Bronze and Iron Age, were used to trap fish in the C19th. The fields now cross the sandbanks beneath the high tide. It was only 500 years ago that Samson was finally separated from Tresco and Bryher and even today on a low Spring tide in August it is perfectly possible to walk across the sands to Tresco and only get wet up to your knees (see photo on p5).

Samson is part of a chain of hills that form the western rim of the islands. They run north to south from Shipman Head to Samson Hill on Bryher, through the twin hills of Samson to Kittern Hill on Gugh. Each hill in this series is crowned with the tombs of the first Scillonians. Its not hard to imagine the attraction of these places to the Bronze Age people - after all we are still attracted to them to watch the sun sink in the west on a Summers evening.

White Island

The ancients must have had a heightened sensitivity to their environment because they lived in much closer and more dependent contact with the landscape than we do. In the later Celtic tradition the whole landscape was almost literally alive. It is perfectly possible that the twin hills were felt to represent the breasts of a mother earth figure. This is a common prehistoric interpretation of such topography and is found in many ancient cultures. A modern day observer glimpsing the setting sun between the twin paps of

Abandoned homes on the South Hill of Samson looking north to Bryher and Tresco

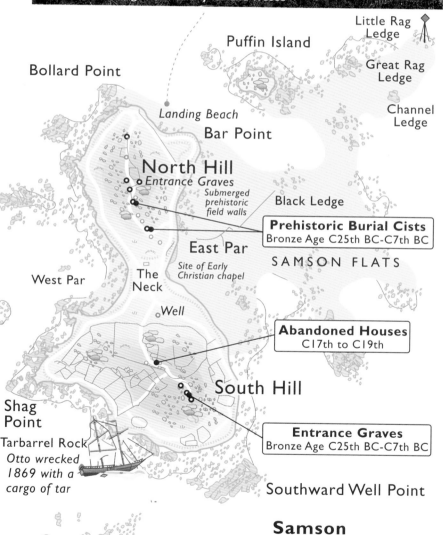

Bollard Point

Puffin Island

Little Rag Ledge

Great Rag Ledge

Channel Ledge

Landing Beach

Bar Point

North Hill

Entrance Graves

Submerged prehistoric field walls

Black Ledge

Prehistoric Burial Cists
Bronze Age C25th BC-C7th BC

East Par

SAMSON FLATS

West Par

The Neck

Site of Early Christian chapel

Well

Abandoned Houses
C17th to C19th

South Hill

Shag Point

Tarbarrel Rock

Otto wrecked 1869 with a cargo of tar

Entrance Graves
Bronze Age C25th BC-C7th BC

Southward Well Point

Great Minalto Ledges

Samson

| 0 | 0.5 | 1km |

| 0 | 1/4 | 1/2 mile |

Southward Well
HMS Colossus wrecked 1798

29

Samson may even experience an ancient stirring in their prehistoric heart.

About 30 years ago a stone lined grave was uncovered on the foreshore of East Porth. It was thought to be associated with the lost chapel of St Sampson. Excavations uncovered a timber structure thought to date from about the C6th. Further north the foundations of a later, rectangular stone building, two graves and a possible stone font were discovered. The later structures would appear to be contemporary with the early Christian sites on St Helen's and Tean.

After a long period of being uninhabited Samson was probably resettled after the Civil War and by the beginning of the C19th about forty people were living here. They seem to have lived in pretty dire circumstances subsisting mostly on potatoes and limpets. Even today you can see the large waste tips of limpet shells outside every house. The island was really too small and its resources were too poor to comfortably support a community. Water was difficult to collect and there was no wood for fuel so the islanders had to rely on collecting bracken and driftwood from the shore. In the early part of the C19th the island was hit by a series of droughts and by the time Augustus Smith took on the lease of the islands in 1834 most of the inhabitants were destitute. Augustus Smith provided housing on St Mary's for those that wanted to move off the island and by 1855 the island was empty. The picturesque decay of the abandoned homes became an inspiration to the poet Tennyson and for the Victorian novel *Armorel of Lyonnesse* by Sir Walter Besant. Samson soon became a popular place to picnic.

The wreck of HMS Colossus

The Colossus was returning from the Mediterranean in November 1798 after being engaged in chasing Napoleon's fleet across the Mediterranean throughout the previous Summer. She took part in the Battle of Cape St Vincent and also in the Battle of the Nile in which Lord Nelson destroyed Napoleon's navy and thwarted his imperial ambitions. The Colossus was badly damaged in the encounter and after the battle retired to Naples for repairs and celebrations. The celebrations and the repairs were short lived. Napoleon's army was approaching Naples and Sir William Hamilton, the British representative to the Court of Naples and husband of the famous Emma was forced to evacuate but not before his wife Lady Emma's heart missed a beat when she met Nelson.

The Colossus was in poor shape, but she was forced to make her weary way under escort to Scilly where she anchored in St Mary's Sound. There followed a week of southerly gales that strained her already damaged fabric and eventually her main anchor cable parted and she was driven onto Southward Well reef. The crew was taken off by local boats but the ship was a complete loss along with Sir William's priceless second collection of Etruscan and Greek pottery (his first makes up the core of the British Museum's collection).

Section 5.

Bryher

Food & Drink

Bryher PO & Stores sells pasties and provisions. Hell Bay Hotel & Fraggle Rock have bar & restaurant. Vine Cafe serves tea & cakes.

Best things to do

Picnic on Gweal Hill & watch the sunset over the Norrard Rocks. Samson Hill has wonderful views.

Ferry

At low water ferries leave from the pontoon on the Bar. At high water ferries leave from Church Quay.

Ferry times and information on the boards at The Town & near the Hell Bay Hotel.

For many people Bryher is the most characteristic island of the whole group. On some days it can be almost frighteningly bleak as waves pile into Hell Bay, but then the next day it can be achingly beautiful and calm. In common with St Agnes the other sentinel on the western edge of the islands, Bryher gets a real bashing in the Winter months. It faces the full force of westerly storms and gales. There is quite a marked division between the northern and southern parts of the island. The southern end is the more sheltered and this is where all the present day inhabitants live.

The northern end is a plateau of exposed high ground, sparsely covered in dwarfed and prostrate heather which hugs the ground to avoid the desiccating winds that sweep across the downs. Shipman Head Down has an exceptional concentration of cairns - man made stone mounds usually built up over an ancient burial although it is thought some may simply be the result of ancient land clearance. In the Bronze Age the climate was going through a mini heat wave which lasted some hundreds of years and areas which today seem exposed and waterlogged were then good agricultural land. Over one hundred cairns are still in existence here, many aligned or linked by low walls. Most have been greatly eroded over the last 3,000 years and at first it can be difficult to distinguish the man made cairns from the surrounding natural rock debris. However, the longer you look the more obvious the cairns become. When your eye is tuned in, you suddenly realise that you are walking in a Bronze Age cemetery where many generations of ancient Scillonians have been buried.

In storms the fetch of the waves that strike Bryher can be as much as 2,000 miles. As the waves arrive in the shallow water west of the island they are slowed by the rough seabed and pile up to a great size. Thousands of tons of water then drop on the coast with every breaker. In bad weather Hell Bay certainly lives up to its name - it becomes a furious caldron of foaming sea and in the worst storms waves will break clean over the top of Shipman Head. At such times the name of nearby Badplace Hill seems comically understated.

The extreme exposure of this part of the island, even within the terms

Looking across New Grimsby harbour to Kitchen Porth

of the Isles of Scilly give it a sense of foreboding even on a calm day. Below Badplace Hill are the remnants of defensive earthworks that formed the landward defensives of Shipman Head Cliff Castle. The headland was fortified in the Iron Age presumably to provide short term shelter to islanders from marauding Irish raiders. The House of the Head cannot help but bring to mind the Iron Age Celts and their cult of head worship. Severed heads were sometimes used to decorate their homes. It always sends a tingle running down my neck.

The southern part of Bryher is partly protected from the worst storms by the Norrard Rocks that lie west of the island and which are best seen from Gweal Hill. On this part of the island there are large sweeping bays backed by sand dunes often punctuated by huge loaf shaped granite outcrops such as Great Carn which children can never resist clambering over - this part of Bryher sometimes seems to be more beach than island. At the very southern tip of the island is the impressive bulk of Samson Hill attached to the rest of Bryher by a low lying sandy neck. It gives the appearance of having been tacked on to the end of Bryher almost as an afterthought. It is as if it had broken away from Samson and slowly drifted north to strand itself on the beaches of Bryher. The hilltop is crowned with two fine entrance graves and there are great views over to the Western and Norrard Rocks. It is especially worth coming up here in the evenings as the sun sets in the west. Below Samson Hill are the lovely intimate bays of Great Porth and Stony Porth.

A prehistoric boundary wall survives on the beach at Green Bay - the large seaweed covered boulders marching into the sea and across the sand flats.

Bryher

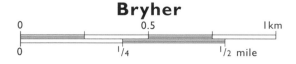

Shipman
Head

House
of the
Head

Tresco

The Gulf

New Grimsby Sound

Smith's Hole

Hole of the Horse

Badplace
Hill

The
Horse

Little Mussel Rock

Boat
Carn

Small Boat
Carn

Great
Bottom

Great Mussel Rock

Castle
Ramparts

The
Bight

Gt. Bottom
Carn

Hell Bay

Bight Drang

Bight
Carn

Anchor Drang

Anchor
Carn

Shipman Head Well Drang

Hangman
Island

Little High Rock Ledge

Cairns

Little High Rock

The Cave

Shipman

Kitchen
Porth

Great High Rock

Head Down

Gt. Rock

Puckie's
Carn

Norrard

Anneka's Quay
(low water landing)

Dunstan's
Rock

Popplestone
Brow

Old Lookout

Watch

Hill

The Bar

Popplestone Neck

Little
Popplestone

The Town

Queen's
Ledge

Black
Carn

Great
Popplestone

Vine Farm

Broomfield
Carn

Gweal
Hill

Little
Pool

New Road

Timmy's
Hill

Church Quay
(high water landing)

Plumb
Island

Silver
Carn

Southward

Community
Centre

T

Wether's
Carn

Great
Pool

Hell Bay
Hotel

Merrick
Island

Prehistoric
submerged
field walls

Stinking
Porth

Hillside
Farm

Veronica
Farm

Green Bay

row
and

Carn
of Bars

Gallery

The Green

on
ck

Merrick
Island

Point
of Bars

South Hill

Brow
Ledges

Three
Brothers

Merrick Island Neck

Gt.
Carn

Great Crabs
Ledge

Great Par

The Brow

Trueboy's
Rocks

Stoneship
Porth

Heathy
Hill

Samson

Little Crabs
Ledge

Touch Rock

Gulf Rock

Western
Carn

Hill

Lubber's
Rock

The Gulf

Riceman's Hole

Entrance
Graves

Bonfire
Carn

Droppy
Nose
Point

Stony Porth

Works
Carn

Rushy
Bay

George's Rock

Sheep
Ledges

Merrick
Island

Works Point

Davey's Rock

South Stony
Porth

Great Rushy
Bay Ledge

Works Carn Entrance Grave
Neolithic/Bronze Age C25th/C5th BC

Middle
Colvel
Rock

Little Rushy Bay Ledge

Outer Colvel Rock

Inner Neck of Gerwick

Bryher Island Walk

The best views are from Watch Hill and Samson Hill. The beaches are the best on the east side of the island but they can feel exposed on a windy day. Kitchen Porth is always more sheltered and has plenty of pools to explore at low water.

Distance: 4 miles round trip (2 hours).

Going: Generally easy along the south of the island. The northern end at Shipman Head Down & Badplace Hill is a little more difficult.

From Church Quay walk a few metres along the road and turn left through a small gap in the sand dunes and onto Green Bay beach.

Green Bay prehistoric field walls

About half way along the beach you will come across a line of large stones disappearing into the water. This is all that remains of a Bronze Age field boundary that has been swamped by the rise in sea levels in the last 3,000 years.

Continue towards the large bulk of Samson Hill.

Samson Hill

Great views to the south and west from the summit. Topped by a number of Bronze Age entrance graves. The best one is on the southern slope of the hill facing Samson.

Great Par

Here a gig shed has been converted into a gallery. The Hell Bay Hotel serves lunches

Great Pool & Gweal Hill

Gweal Hill is great place to watch the sun set over the Western and Norrard Rocks.

If you want to return to the east side of the island use the footpath that runs inland from Great Popplestone under Puckie's Carn. To continue the round island walk follow the coastal path.

Shipman Head Down

On the surface of the down are an almost unprecedented concentration of cairns - prehistoric burial mounds.

Cliff Castle & Badplace Hill

You may be able to just make out the remains of a bank and ditch across the neck of the headland. The area was used as a cliff castle from the Iron Age. It also probably served as a temporary refuge from Viking marauders in the early Medieval period.

It is possible to cross the Gulf to Shipman Head via the neck of slippery rocks. Watch the tide though or you will be marooned on the House of the Head.

Shipman Head

Beyond the shelter of Scilly Rock and the Norrard Rocks this headland takes the full brunt of Atlantic storms. Waves break over the top in severe storms.

Hangman's Island & Kitchen Porth

Hangman's island is said to have been used to hang mutinous sailors. The jib is modern.

The Bar

Main landing place at low water when Church Quay drys out. Before the construction of the pontoon passengers used to have to walk the plank from the bow of the boat onto the sand. The new pontoon was built as part of the Challenge Anneka television series.

Section 6.
Tresco

Tresco is leased from the Duchy of Cornwall by the Dorrien-Smith family who live in Tresco Abbey. It is the only island on Scilly that retains this old relationship that once saw the whole group leased firstly, to the Godolphin family and then in the C19th to Augustus Smith. As proprietor of the islands, his humane and far sighted approach revitalised the poverty struck islands. He introduced new agricultural methods and developed the flower and tourism industries. Emphasis was placed on the importance of education for the children of Scilly and he funded the building of schools on the islands. It was Augustus Smith who started the Abbey Gardens - now famous throughout the world for their sub-tropical plants and beautiful setting.

Tresco Abbey has its origins in the C12th. Henry I granted all the religious establishments on northern Scilly (they were then one single isle) to the Benedictine monks of Tavistock Abbey. The Abbey - properly a priory was dedicated to St Nicholas. Gauging from the fragmentary remains of the priory church it was a substantial building by Scillonian standards, although it was probably home to only a handful of monks at any one time. Scilly was very vulnerable to raids by pirates and Vikings. The priory and chapels would have been especially tempting targets. In the Viking Orkneyinga saga Scilly is mentioned as an easy target and details of a raid are recounted. The monks didn't take it all lying down though, they had their own zero tolerance policy. In 1209 they are supposed to have beheaded 120 pirates in one afternoon. It was probably a rare victory and the monks finally abandoned Tresco in the C14th after about 300 years of occupation.

The remains of the church now form the framework for one of the most delightful gardens in the country. In common with many gardens in Cornwall the Abbey Gardens are at their best in the Spring and early Summer. The whole garden is protected by a belt of trees that were originally planted by Augustus Smith - up to that point there were no trees growing on Tresco. Many of these trees were blown down in a series of storms that culminated in the hurricane of 1990. Since then over 60,000 replacement trees have be planted to reestablish the shelter belt. Many of the original plants were purchased from passing sailing ships returning to Britain from the southern hemisphere. The beautiful blue Agapanthus are native to South Africa and

Cork Porth

Piper's
Hole Cave

Old Grimsby Sound

Coal Ledge

Kettle
Point

Gun Hole

Gun
Hill

Gun Well

Gimble
Point

Tregarthen
Hill

Cairns

Entrance
Graves

North
End

Little
Kittern

Coal
Porth

Gimble
Porth

Castle Down
Brow

Merchant's
Point

Raven's
Rock

Crow's
Island

King Charles'
Castle

Gimble
Point

Peashopper
Island

Pollock
Rock

Cairns

Merchant's
Rock

Middle
Carn

Island
Hotel

Long Ledge

Cromwell's
Castle

Castle
Porth

Castle
Down

Beacon
Hill

Norrard

Porth Mellin

Long Point

Tide
Rock

Frenchman's
Point

Old
Lookout

Hotel
Beach

Quay

Old Grimsby

Braiden
Rock

Back Lane

Ray Island

Green
Porth

Block House Point

Cook's Bar

New Grimsby Harbour

Dial
Rocks

Townshill

School &
Community
Centre

Blockhouse

Cook's
Porth

Crad
Poin

Point
Carn

New
Grimsby

Dolphin
House

Dolphin
Town

Blockhouse
Cottages

Anneka's Quay
(low water landing)

T

The Palace
Gallery

New Inn

Borough Road

Bryher

New Grimsby
(high water landing)

Timothy's
Corner

Vane
Hill

Racket
Town
Carn

The Warren
Cliff Cottage

Bay
Row

Racket Town Lane

Borough
Farm

Old Seaplane Slip

Farm Beach

Abbey
Farm

Estate
Office

Pool Road

Middle Down

Parting
Carn

Church Quay
(high water landing)

Plumb
Island

Saffron
Cove

Sluice Gate

Bird
Hide

Bird Hide

Pentle
House

Merrick
Island

Green Bay

Plumb
Rocks

Plumb
Hill

Great Pool

Three
Brothers

Great Crabs
Ledge

Abbey Drive

Little Crabs
Ledge

Abbey Wood

Abbey
Hill

Abbey
Garden

T

Tresco Abbe

Lubber's
Rock

Penzance Road

Abbey Pool

Appletree Point

Appletree
Carn

Abbey Green

Great Rock

TRESCO FLATS

Appletree
Bay

Appletree
Banks

Figtree
Rocks

Crab's Le

Tresco

Rushy
Bank

Sea Carn

Bathinghouse
Porth

0   0.5   1km

Prehistoric
submerged
field walls

Figtree
Ledge

Broad
Ledge

0   1/4   1/2 mile

Puffin Island

Little Rag
Ledge

Chinks

Oliver's
Battery

Carn Near Quay
(low water landing)

Great Rag
Ledge

Carn Near

Yello
Ledg

36

Channel
Ledge

Long Crow

Crow Point

Hulman

Cromwell's Castle, Tresco

shy Point

Rushy
Porth

Tea Ledge

Channel Rocks

Lizard Point

Pentle Bay

Great Pentle
Rock

Skirt Island

Diamond Ledge

Cones

Green
Island

Tobaccoman's Ledge

Tobaccoman's Point

the Echeiums are more commonly found in the Canary Isles. The Abbey Gardens are also of interest to the non gardener because amongst the shrubs are a number of interesting artifacts gathered from the surrounding islands. The most ancient is a Bronze Age holed stone or menhir. There is a Romano-British inscribed stone and most interestingly, a Roman shrine found in a well beneath the Garrison wall. The side panels of the shrine have carved reliefs of a dagger and an axe indicting that it was probably a sacrificial altar. With the shrine at Nornour on the Eastern Isles this suggests Scilly was on a Roman trade route. At Valhalla there is a collection of figureheads from ships wrecked on the islands plus the brazier that was used to illuminate the old lighthouse on St Agnes.

There is plenty to see on the rest of the island after a visit to the gardens. The south of Tresco is covered with softly undulating sand dunes that are cloaked with wild flowers in the Spring and Summer. North of a line drawn between Old Grimsby and New Grimsby are the exposed cliffs of Castle Down.

New Grimsby Harbour is a favoured anchorage on Scilly and yachts often moor here in the Summer. In the days of sail ships it was the preferred anchorage in the islands because its protected from gales by the high ground on either side and has good holding ground for anchors. It is quite a confined space for a sailing ship and getting in and out could be a problem if the wind was light or from the wrong quarter. There are giant iron rings fixed to the rocks at the mouth of the Sound and these were used to pull and steady ships as they entered or left the harbour. King Charles' Castle was built on Castle Down in 1550 to protect the haven from the threat of invasion by the French and Spanish. At the same time the Blockhouse was built to protect Old Grimsby Sound and the deep water St Helen's Pool. After the end of the English Civil War in 1648 Scilly took part in an uprising against Parliament and for a time the islands became a base for privateers and pirates. This so upset the Dutch that they declared war on the islands and sent a fleet of ships under Admiral Van Tomp to take the islands. Fearful that the islands would fall to a foreign power, Parliament sent its own force under Admiral Blake to subdue the rebels and defend the islands. He landed on the north of Tresco and set up defences at Oliver's Battery at Carn Near halting the resupply of the Star Castle which soon capitulated. King Charles' Castle was then replaced in 1651 by Cromwell's Castle. This was better sited at sea level in order to deter enemy shipping from entering New Grimsby Sound.

Tresco Island Walk

Distance: 5 miles round trip for the whole island circuit (about 3¹/₂ hours).
Going: Generally easy along south of the island - can also be walked along the beach at low water. The more rugged northern end of the island is a more typical cliff path walk. **Pub/Refreshments:** Pub lunch at New Inn. Cafe at New Grimsby Quay and refreshments from the Abbey Gardens (entrance fee) & Island Hotel.

Cromwell's Castle
Until the Medieval period New Grimsby Sound was the main anchorage in the islands. The castle was constructed in 1651 to guard the main approach.

King Charles' Castle
Built before Cromwell's Castle in 1550, but was poorly sited and eventually superseded by Cromwell's Castle. Associated with extensive defensive groundworks which have been reinstated in recent years.

Piper's Hole
Large cave with an internal pool that goes back 50 metres into the cliffs.

Tregarthen Hill
Fine entrance grave on the southern side of the summit. There are views over to Round Island and St Martin's and its a good spot to take a picnic.

Blockhouse
Built to protect the anchorage of St Helen's Pool in 1554 at the same time as King Charles' Castle and held by the Royalists during the English Civil War.

Pentle Bay & Bathinghouse Porth
A number of submerged prehistoric hut circles and boundary walls are sometimes evident on the foreshore at Pentle Bay and Bathinghouse Porth - see map. Look out for the straight alignment of the boundary walls among the other boulders on the foreshore. The layer of peat that shows in the intertidal zone is evidence of the submergence of fields. You can sometimes see the remains of hut circles at Bathinghouse Porth but this is dependent on the level of sand cover.

You can shortcut back to New Grimsby via Pool Lane.

Abbey Farm
The buildings and slip here were established as a base for flying boats in both the World War I & II. Their principal tasks were to hunt down U-Boats prowling the Western Approaches and to rescue downed pilots. The slip still survives.

Section 7.
Tean, St Helen's & Round Island

All the islands in this northern part of Scilly are now uninhabited but were once home to at least two Celtic Christian saints. Inter-island ferries do not make regular landings here but will make special trips on request.

Tean (pronounced Tee-an)
This small island is the site of an Iron Age settlement and an early C8th Christian chapel. Hut circles and ancient field walls have been identified in the sandy bays of East and West Porth and in St Helen's Porth. Great Hill has an entrance grave as does the Old Man. The most well known site is St Theona's Chapel. When the site was excavated sixteen early Christian graves were found under the east wall of the small rectangular stone chapel. This showed the chapel to be from a later period than the earliest graves. They were probably dug at a time when the original wooden chapel was still standing over 1,000 years ago. It is thought that the graves are those of the founders of the site - one of which is the grave of St Theona herself. Unfortunately very little if anything is known of St Theona. It is assumed that Theona was a woman - and certainly women saints are common in the Celtic nations. The site may have been occupied at the same time as St Elidius's chapel on St Helen's and there were probably similar chapels on Samson, St Martin's and St Agnes.

St Helen's
The name St Helen's is actually a corruption of St Elidius who was an obscure Celtic saint. The remains of an early Christian Chapel and circular hermit cell are thought to date from the C8th. A similar structure has been uncovered at Perranporth in north Cornwall and many of the established churches in Cornwall probably started in the same way as St Elidius' chapel. Of Elidius we know little, except that he was said to be the son of a British king and a bishop in the early church.

St Elidius may have lived in the small circular cell. The site seems to have kept growing in religious importance and in the C11th about 300 years after the death of Elidius, a small church was built. At the same time a number of smaller rectangular buildings were constructed. They presumably housed the men and women who cared for the site. Inside the chapel is an altar with a hidden recess for holy relics of Elidius and a grave in the church is thought to belong to the man himself. The church was extended and embellished probably by the monks of Tavistock Abbey soon after they settled on Tresco in the C12th. The site fell into disuse and ruin in the C14th or C15th. A service is still held on the island on August 6th each year to celebrate the feast day of St Elidius. A display board at the site gives a detailed history of the ruins and has pictures of some of the artifacts found during the excavations. They are now housed in the Island Museum in Hugh Town on St Mary's.

On the southern side of the island lies a ruined rectangular building. It is usually referred to as the *Pest House* and is an C18th isolation building used to quarantine sailors landed from disease ridden ships. It continued the St Helen's tradition for hermits and isolation but in this case it was enforced isolation. To the west of the island lies a wide reef called the Golden Ball Brow which has claimed numerous ships. Its last victim was the Panamanian ship *Mando* in January 1955. When wind and tide conditions are right surfers sometimes wait here for the large freak waves that occasionally hit the reef.

Round Island

West Landing   Ea

Camber Rocks

Men-a-vaur

Golden Ball

Didley Point

St Helen's

Golden Ball Brow

We
Ga
Roc

The Pest House
Isolation Hospital C18th

Landing Carn

Beef Neck

St Elidius's Chapel
Early Christian C8th

Coal Ledge

Coal Porth

St Helen's Pool

Little Kittern

Northwethel

Old Grimsby Sound

Gimble Porth

Merchant's Point

Round Rock

Gimble Point

Raven's Rock

Crow's Island

Foremans Island

Merchant's Rock

Peashopper Island

Tean, St Helen's & Round Island

Middle Ledge

0   0.5   1km

0   1/4   1/2 ile

Hotel Beach

Norrard

Tide Rock

Round Island from Tresco

Round Island

The lighthouse was built in 1887 and completed a ring of lighthouses that mark the Isles of Scilly from all parts of the compass. Its height of almost 70 metres above sea level often allows the light to be seen from the Land's End Peninsula, almost 30 miles away. The lighthouse is now automated as are all the lights around Scilly and Lands End. The island stands right on the edge of deep water and waves pile up as they suddenly hit the shallows. A storm in 1886 was found to have washed limpets and stones on to the roof of the accommodation building 60 metres above sea level.

Pollard

s Gap

Glory Hole

East Gap Rock

Pednbrose

Pednbream

Tean Sound

Porth Seal

Cheese Corner

Black Porth

St Helen's Porth

Great Hill

Tinkler's Rock

Tean

Tinkler's Hill

West Porth
Submerged prehistoric field walls

Goat's Point

St Martin's Hotel

Old Lookout

ld
lan

East Porth

Yellow Carn
Yellow Carn Porth

Point of Fields

Shaken Rock

Clodgie Point

St Martin's

St Theona's Chapel
Early Christian C8th

Crump Island

Southward Carn

Neck of the Pool

Hedge Rock

Hedge Rock Ledge

John Martin's Ledge

Section 8.
St Martin's & The Eastern Isles

Food & Drink
Post Office & shop at Higher Town. St Martin's Hotel restaurant for evening meals. Cafe in Higher Town. Seven Stones Inn at Lower Town. **Best things to do** Explore Chapel Down. Good views from Cruther's Hill over Crow Bar to St Mary's & from Chapel Brow to the Sevenstones reef.
Ferry
Most ferries will call at both Higher Town and Lower Town quays. At low water boats tend to come into the hotel quay at Lower Town.

St Martin's makes up the north eastern limit of Scilly and is the most picturesque of all the islands. Seen from the air it forms a distinctive crescent shape, with a spine of high ground that curves along the centre of the whole island from Chapel Down in the east, to White Island in the north. More than any other island in the group St Martin's is an island of sweeping bays. Almost all of the cultivated land runs down from the spine of the island to the south and western coasts that overlook Crow Sound and the sand banks of St Martin's Flats. This side of the island with its sunny aspect is covered with tiny sheltered flower and vegetable fields. Wild Agapanthus, Lily and Hottentot Fig grow from every hedge and wall and dunes run down to the waterside, softening the whole coastline. The sheltered, lush scallop shaped bays of Higher Town and Lawrance's Bay run down to soft dunes.

The northeast side of the island makes a nice contrast especially the magnificent St Martin's Bay. This side of the island in uncultivated, weather beaten, wind blasted and exposed - a bulwark to the North Atlantic.

The islanders' forefathers showed commendable brevity in naming the three main settlements as Higher, Middle and Lower Town. This no nonsense attitude to place-names is a delightful understatement that could only work on Scilly. It's a practice that St Martin's also shares with St Agnes, the most south westerly island of the group.

There are many good archaeological sites on the island. A Bronze Age statue menhir has been repositioned on the south of Chapel Down. The face is now ill defined, but in the right sort of oblique light its features can be made out although this is tricky unless you catch the sun in exactly the right position. If you really want to see the facial features it is best go up at night with a torch to shine across the face perhaps then continuing to St Martin's Head to watch the eight lighthouses whose lights are visible from here. An alignment of entrance graves crowns Cruther's Hill and echo similar groupings on the western rim of the islands at Gugh and Samson.

Further northwest, there is a entrance grave on Knackyboy Carn. There is not much to see now, but it was excavated in the 1950's and found to be almost undisturbed by grave robbers. Seventy pottery urns were found in the chamber. They contained cremated bones and amber beads and brooches.

It is unusual to find a tomb that has not been robbed of its contents.

An early Christian chapel once stood below the daymark on Chapel Down and the rectangular foundations are visible early in the season before the bracken smothers them. It was probably built to show a light to guide shipping in the early Medieval period. It was common practice for religious houses to set up lights on the highest headlands often manned only by a solitary monk. Almost all the prominent headlands in Britain are named after a saint for this reason. The chapel was robbed of stone during the construction of the daymark and Napoleonic signal station that stand on Chapel Brow. The signal station used a semaphore system to communicate with naval vessels standing offshore ready to pounce on any passing 'Frenchie'. It was replaced after only a few years service by a purpose built tower at Telegraph on St Mary's.

It is worth a scramble across the rocks for a visit to White Island. The only slate rock on the otherwise granite islands is on the extreme north of the island. It is the only remnant of sediment from the Laurasian Mountains that once stood 5 miles high above the granite. The presence of the granite is an indication that a collision of continental plates took place to the south. The suture line between the plates runs along the line of the English Channel.

An entrance grave lies on the north of the island and a kelp pit sits just above the beach at Porth Morran. In the C17th and C18th a family from Falmouth called Nance started a cottage industry cutting seaweed to turn into kelp. The seaweed was cut, dried on the shore then burnt in the shallow stone lined pits to produce a dark green mass of kelp. Soda and potash were then extracted for use in the glass and soap industries. The end product gave old glass its characteristic green hue. This was a widespread industry on the western seaboard of Britain.

The process gave off copious amounts of noxious smoke and was unpopular with many of the inhabitants of the islands. It was never anything but a subsistence industry - but it was a period when island incomes were very low and poverty was rife. It took about 20 tons of seaweed (principally oar weed) to produce just one ton of kelp and must have been backbreaking work.

The Eastern Isles

A collection of small uninhabited and sheltered islands south of St Martin's. They are a favourite place for seals who haul themselves onto the rocks to bask in the sun. Grey seals spend most of their lives at sea but come inshore to moult and breed on the Eastern Isles. September and October are the main breeding months. The cows are able to give an exceptionally rich milk that allows the pups to gain 9 kilos in the first week after birth. After three weeks the pup is abruptly deserted by its mother and over the next two weeks and it lives off it's fat while the sea coat grows. At this time the cows will mate again but the fertilised egg will be not develop until the Spring.

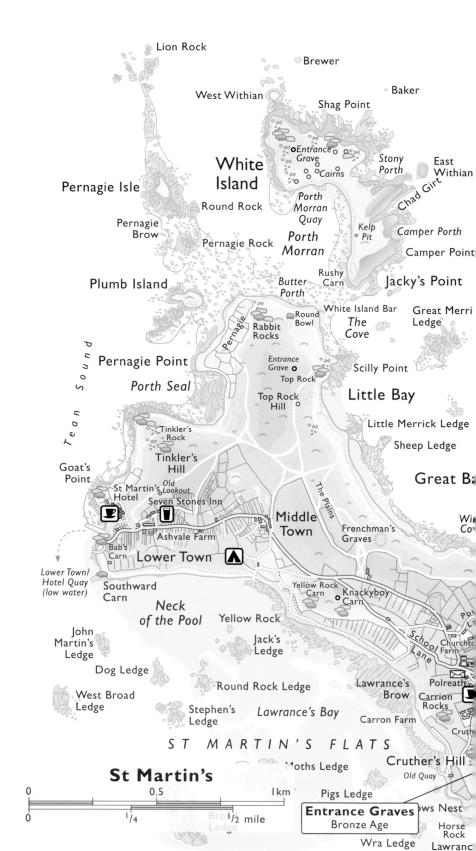

Lion Rock

Brewer

Baker

West Withian

Shag Point

White
Island

Entrance
Grave

Cairns

Stony
Porth

East
Withian

Pernagie Isle

Round Rock

Porth
Morran
Quay

Chad Girt

Camper Porth

Pernagie
Brow

Pernagie Rock

Porth
Morran

Kelp
Pit

Camper Point

Plumb Island

Butter
Porth

Rushy
Carn

Jacky's Point

Tean Sound

Pernagie

Rabbit
Rocks

Round
Bowl

White Island Bar

The
Cove

Great Merri
Ledge

Pernagie Point

Entrance
Grave

Scilly Point

Porth Seal

Top Rock

Little Bay

Top Rock
Hill

Little Merrick Ledge

Tinkler's
Rock

Sheep Ledge

Goat's
Point

Tinkler's
Hill

Great B:

St Martin's
Hotel

Old
Lookout

Seven Stones Inn

The Plains

Middle
Town

Frenchman's
Graves

Wi
Co

Ashvale Farm

Bab's
Carn

Lower Town

Lower Town/
Hotel Quay
(low water)

Southward
Carn

Neck
of the Pool

Yellow Rock

Yellow Rock
Carn

Knackyboy
Carn

Po

John
Martin's
Ledge

Jack's
Ledge

School Lane

Churchto
Farm

Dog Ledge

Round Rock Ledge

Lawrance's
Brow

Polreath

Carrion
Rocks

West Broad
Ledge

Stephen's
Ledge

Lawrance's Bay

Carron Farm

Cruth

S T   M A R T I N ' S   F L A T S

Moths Ledge

Cruther's Hill

St Martin's

Old Quay

0 _____ 0.5 _____ 1km

0 _____ 1/4 _____ 1/2 mile

Bro__
Ledge

Pigs Ledge

ws Nest

Entrance Graves
Bronze Age

Horse
Rock

Wra Ledge

Lawranc
Le

The bulls are more conspicuous than the cows because of their darker coats and larger size. The seals return in January and February to moult and allow their new sea coats to grow.

Most of the islands are covered by bracken from mid Summer onwards, so those wishing to see the archaeological remains should try to get to the isles in the first part of the year. Just above the beach on Nornour is a settlement of Iron Age courtyard houses - a more elaborate form of roundhouse

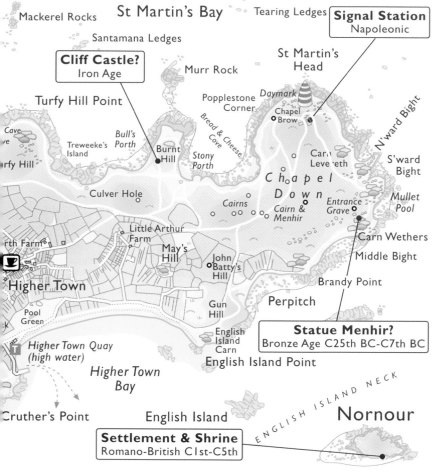

Mackerel Rocks

St Martin's Bay

Tearing Ledges

Signal Station
Napoleonic

Santamana Ledges

Cliff Castle?
Iron Age

Murr Rock

St Martin's
Head

Turfy Hill Point

Popplestone
Corner

Daymark

Chapel
Brow

N'ward Bight

Cave
ve

Treweeke's
Island

Bull's
Porth

Burnt
Hill

Stony
Porth

Bread & Cheese
Cove

Carn
Leve eth

S'ward
Bight

rfy Hill

Culver Hole

C h a p e l
D o w n

Mullet
Pool

Cairns

Cairn &
Menhir

Entrance
Grave

Little Arthur
Farm

Carn Wethers

rth Farm

May's
Hill

John
Batty's
Hill

Middle Bight

Higher Town

Gun
Hill

Brandy Point

Pool
Green

Perpitch

k

Higher Town Quay
(high water)

English
Island
Carn

Statue Menhir?
Bronze Age C25th BC-C7th BC

English Island Point

Higher Town
Bay

Cruther's Point

English Island

E N G L I S H   I S L A N D   N E C K

Nornour

Settlement & Shrine
Romano-British C1st-C5th

45

with workrooms and store rooms around the sides of an open courtyard (see illustration on page 14). Nornour is a significant settlement in the history of the islands. It was founded in the Bronze Age but during the Roman period was expanded and may have been used as a shrine by mariners. Hundreds of fine brooches, pins, glass beads and jewellery have been found here along with Roman coins and other religious offerings. It may have also been the site of the main harbour on the islands in the Roman period. Another important find is a clay figurine, probably of the Roman goddess Venus. Finds from Nornour are exhibited in the museum on St Mary's.

On the foreshore of Nornour are the rusting boilers of the passenger paddle steamer Earl of Aran. In July 1862, she hit Irishman's Ledge just east of Nornour after the captain took the advice of a local man to take a short cut to St Mary's through English Island Neck.
Woops.

Grey Seal

Hanjague

English Island Neck

Great English Island Ledge **Nornour**

English Island

Settlement & Shrine
Romano-British C1st-C5th

Irishman's Ledge

Nornour Brow

Northward Head

Shag Rocks

Round Rock

Earl of Aran wrecked 1872. Boiler shows at low water

Jolly Point

Great Ganilly

Mou

Ganilly Bar

Holmbush Carn

East Porth

Little Innisvouls

Inner Scud

Little Ganilly

West Porth

Innisvouls Brow

Western Scud

Seal Rock

Innisvouls Neck

Long Scud

Little Arthur

Outer Carn

Great Ganinick

Eastward Guthern

Little Ganilly Neck

Ladies Ledge

Great Innisvouls

Great Ledge

Ladies Ledge

Menawethan Nec

Middle Arthur

Entrance Graves

Ragged Island

Menaweth

Ganinick Brow

Sheep Carn

Arthur Porth

Arthur Brow

Cadedna Ledges

Renny

The Hole
The Peak

Chi
Poi

Little Ganinick

Frenchman's Rock

Great Arthur

Arthur Head

Eastern Isles

0   0.5   1km

0   1/4   1/2 mile

St Martin's Island Walk

The island is split into two parallel and curved strips. The south and west facing coasts are cultivated and easy to walk. The north and west coast are more wild and bleak and are slightly harder going.

Distance: A complete circuit of the island is about 6 miles (3 hours). If you don't want to do the whole circuit stroll up to Chapel Down & then walk back across the spine of the island. **Going:** Generally easy on the south of the island. **Pub/Refreshments:** Sevenstones Pub at Lower Town. Tea & cakes at Higher Town & at St Martin's Hotel.

From Higher Town Quay follow the coast path over the dunes towards English Island Point.

Chapel Down Menhir

In the middle of a cairn above Carn Wethers is a small menhir or standing stone. There is a barely recognizable face carved into the stone. The features are much more apparent when the light falls obliquely on the face, or alternatively take a torch up at dusk.

St Martin's Head Daymark & Chapel

The daymark was erected in the C17th. The rectangular buildings are the remains of a Napoleonic signal station. Messages were relayed to ships off shore by semaphore. Below the daymark and usually obscured by vegetation, are the scant remains of an early Christian chapel. It was probably an early lighthouse run by a religious order. Look northeast and you may see waves breaking over the Sevenstones Reef - the grave of the Torrey Canyon in 1967.

Frenchman's Graves

Said to be the burial ground of a whole ship's crew wrecked on the rocks below. Cliff burial was common practice in the C17th and C18th for bodies washed ashore after a wreck. It was especially true for those thought to be the bodies of Frenchmen who had the temerity to be at the same time Catholic, Republican & French - not a popular recipe at the time.

Burnt Hill Cliff Castle

Thought to be the remains of a minor cliff castle or settlement from the Iron Age. The promontory is protected by low wall on the landward side. The outline of two round houses can just be made out inside the enclosure.

White Island

Accessible at low water only. The very northern tip of the island is composed of the only remnant of slate rock on Scilly. A fine entrance grave sits on the high ground to the north of the island and there is a good example of a kelp pit sitting just above the beach at Porth Morran.

Cruther's Hill

At the summit there is an alignment of entrance graves. Good view back towards Tresco and St Mary's over Crow Bar. At the time the entrance graves were constructed, they would have looked over fields and woods and not over sea as today. The people whose remains were deposited in the tombs probably farmed this now submerged land.

Knackyboy Carn

Just behind the carn are the remains of an excavated entrance grave which revealed a series of pottery urns filled with cremated human remains.

Plants of Scilly

Stonecrop

Sea Campion

Like all islands the flora of Scilly is dominated by specialist maritime plants. The granite soils are generally poor in nutrients but it is loss of moisture that is the major problem for any plant in this exposed habitat. A whole ecosystem of specialised plants and animals have adapted to turn this problem to their advantage. Most are adapted to increase their ability to retain precious water and in this respect they adopt the same sort of strategies as desert plants - small, waxy, fleshy leaves to reduce transpiration and store water; low growing, dwarfed or prostrate habits where the wind is slower and where ground cover reduces the drying out of the soil and a short growing season triggered by favourable conditions. In fact many are often so completely adapted they are unable to grow or compete in more fertile, sheltered areas. These specialists are a delight to any plant lover.

Plants of the cliff & down

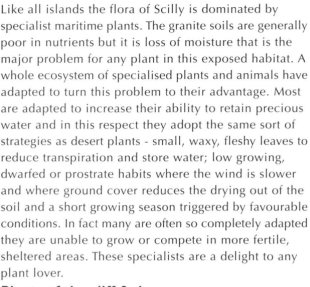

Thrift

Western Gorse

Common Centaury

Inhospitable headlands and exposed granite carns crown all the islands. Perhaps the most noticeable feature of the granite carns is the luxuriant growth of the green bearded lichen ramalina. It often completely cloaks the massive granite boulders and obviously luxuriates in the clean, moist atmosphere of Scilly. On the same headlands thrift or sea pink is often found growing out of the smallest fissure in the bare rock. On the more sheltered carns sea campion, danish scurvy grass and samphire compete with the thrift and sea mayweed is often found in sheltered corners in the Summer. On the cliffs english stonecrop grows on the slightest area of weathered granite and in the short turf common centaury and sea carrot are often found. As shelter increases the turf gives way to bracken. In Spring a woodland type ecosystem flourishes here - bluebells, violets and brambles take advantage of the light before the bracken shades them out in the Summer. The brambles are the bane of anyone pushing through the bracken to find archaeological sites which are all but lost by August. On the windswept downs a thin soil allows gnarled, stunted prostrate Heathers to grow often accompanied by lousewort a hemi-parasite growing off the roots of the heather. Western gorse dominates wide areas of the Downs. Its yellow pea flowers open all year round. They have a wonderful almost overpowering coconut scent on still Spring days.